Olivia Dedman is a poet, ⌐ youth homelessness, living a⌐ Peterborough Poet Laureate⌐ performs for and works with o⌐ around the UK, such as Metal C⌐ Eastern Angles Theatre and Cᴿ⌐ᴸ ᴹⁱⁿᵈ. ᴾʳᵉᵛⁱᵒᵘˢˡʸ ᵖᵘᵇˡⁱˢʰᵉᵈ in Eastside's *I Know, I Wish, I Will* and Nottingham C.A.N's *I Come From* anthologies. *bodies, beds & heads* is Olivia's debut poetry collection.

bodies, beds & heads

Olivia Dedman

Bx3

This edition published by Bx3, an imprint of Burning Eye Books 2021

www.burningeye.co.uk

@burningeyebooks

Burning Eye Books
15 West Hill, Portishead, BS20 6LG

ISBN 978-1-913958-13-8

for Karen

Contents

bodies

beds

heads

bodies

girls

girls

                                    wear pink
                            they have long hair
                            they don't think

pretty girls

                                wear makeup
                            and starve to shrink

girly girls

                                are blonde
                                and small
                            they don't brawl

nice girls

                                play barbies
                        and they don't sprawl
                    they sit politely on the floor
                            they don't spit
                                    or hit
    and they only kiss the boys that tease them

good girls

                        don't speak out of turn
                            they cross their legs
                                they're seen
                                and not heard

naughty girls

                        don't do as they're told
                                slutty girls
                        open their legs for anyone
                    they leave nothing to the imagination

frigid girls

                                are stuck-up
                                    virgins
                                fake girls
                    should embrace their natural beauty

ugly girls

                        would look better with some lippy

psycho bitch girls

                        check their boyfriends' phones

gym bunny girls

count their macros

career girls

are baby-hating crows

curvy girls

are whales promoting obesity

skinny girls

are disgusting
and need a sandwich

bimbo girls

are all fake tits
and bleached hair
desperate girls
are wedding-obsessed freaks

girls

should go to work

girls

don't want to be left on the shelf

girls

have a body clock

girls

shouldn't wear short skirts
if they don't want to be touched

girls

are apples, pears, hourglass
diamonds
triangular, spoons

girls

these days
are selfie-obsessed
skin-injecting
sex-selling
clones

but girls

these days
don't know how lucky they are
that they can vote

puppy fat

sticking the word
puppy
in front of
fat
doesn't make me feel less fat
and sticking the word
just
in front of that
still doesn't make me feel less
fat

I wore shorts

each day was the same
mornings sweating in dirty memories
the sun's glare flashing
through sleepy blinks
my vision was stained by his clicking shutter

he paved my way to school
anxiety dancing a fidgety hopscotch over cracks
his biro-doodled face etched into my mind
the long-lasting scribe
of what my hand drew for police that night

I drew what I couldn't speak
worry roads crossing with bursts of my body
being shared as a hobby

they stayed awake with me
in my bed
the shadowy men
silhouettes
lit up by their screens flashing my ten-year-old body

my routine had changed
and I wore shorts after him
no more skirts
jean shorts with belts done up tight
cycling shorts that clung to my thighs
shorts under skirts as a disappointing surprise

My Grandad's Chip Pan

Grease is a common ingredient of the working-class tea.
It hangs itself as spatters on cracked kitchen tiles
and congeals comfortably in the crevices of the wooden
    tables and chairs.
My grandad's chip pan was moved to the shed
after it became too tedious for my gran to scrub the build-up
    of grease coating the kitchen each day.
From the garden, he'd shout,
    'Come help Grandad peel the taters.'
My grandad would sit me on the garden stool.
He'd roll up the sleeve of my silver puffer coat and,
with numb fingertips, we'd swipe the thick muddied skins with
    a blade.
Before pressing start on the microwaved peas, my gran would
    say,
    'Go and see if Grandad's chips are nearly done.'
and I'd make the short run back to the shed that bellowed the
    smell of chip pan chips covered in grease.
My gran would make a bed for them
with folded-up squares of kitchen roll and they'd lie there,
dripping oil onto the fresh sheets,
before being piled on our plates.
We had sausages, peas and Grandad's chips for tea at eight.

Tiny Dancers

The waif with the straight hair perches on a bench,
twiddling her mother's Mercedes keys between her fingertips
and tranced in unconscious privilege.
Resentment peeks from behind my stare
as the hairdressing mother yanks back my head.
She slaps at my unruly curls
with my own mum's sticky green gel that she got cheap from Lidl.
I'm drenched in her coffee breath as she mutters,
    'Your hair has a life of its own…'
and she deflates me with fifty borrowed bobby pins.
Miss orders me into the draughty cupboard with some other girls
to take off our knickers.
    'It looks sloppy,'
so, breezy bare,
I rejoin the line and smooth my escaping baby hairs.
In the hall,
we stand stiff in front of the panel and our wrists twist into bras bas.
Four withered frames,
arms and necks embellished in throbbing, snaking veins, wait.
They rest their bony hands on the big oak desk.
The one in the middle pushes her glasses up her spindly nose
and nods to Miss.
The breath trapped in my lungs makes my muscles shake
until I exhale
when she presses play on the tape
and we sway,
lurching to display
the graceful robotics of the Royal Ballet.

my skin blotched when I denied a lollipop

and I collapsed
when I opened my eyes
my head had been thrust between my thighs
and I was hooked

A Scotch Pancake & a Funsize Mars Bar

One day,
inside the peeling multicoloured-roofed building,
through the five locked doors
and in a room that said

IN USE

I stared at the ceiling.
Brown Boots the counsellor,
her feet sweating in boots and socks in summer,
read my recent stats and muttered
about how I wasn't sticking to the plan or some other bollocks.
I looked down from the ceiling and locked her eyes,
deadpan expression on my face.
I shrugged and said,
     'Dunno.'
Brown Boots told me there were three options for my future.
I could
     a. stick to the plan
     b. get locked up as an inpatient
     c. die
so I agreed to eating
a Scotch pancake for breakfast and a funsize Mars bar after tea.

Wankbank

Four missed nudges 'cause you've BRB'd to eat your tea and now Jamie from DT has popped up in a new window, sniggering, saying he's got your tits in pixelated printer ink in front of him. You tell him you don't believe him but your chicken dippers and chips are curdling in that dreaded feeling, now your stomach's sinking. Jamie sends you the file and it takes a while to download through your Limewire viruses but the emoji in your nickname still smiles. In the file, you file through photos of girls you know from school until you see your own face staring back and Jamie says he got it off Tom and Jack and that your body's so fit he'd tap that and that he'll put you in his wankbank.

I Can't Piss

I leave PE,
bloody desperate for a wee.
In the cubicle, I can finally release.
No piss.
With a burning bladder,
I manage to squeeze a trickle,
and I go back to PE still needing a wee.

After school, I'm late to meet him
because I'm back in the toilet trying to piss.

I fuck fucking off and fuck him off because I made him wait
and I can't give him nothing in the end.
But I couldn't give a fuck because I still can't piss.

Now I'm in the safety of my own toilet
and there's nothing like your own toilet
so I get ready to enjoy it.
I squeeze again:
one fiery droplet.
My forehead is hot from straining.
I cry in pain.

What if I can't ever piss again?
                    I must be a freak.
          Something's wrong with my body
                    Is this a symptom of pregnancy?

Google tells me it's cancer, probably.
I tell Mum
    'Nothing'
when she asks me what's wrong.
But my screwed-up face gives me away
and I gush,
    'I can't piss.'

Mum says,
    'That sounds like a UTI,'
and I say,
    'Will I die?'

In the walk-in clinic,
the nurse says,
    'It's just an infection in the urinary tract.'
Thank fuck for that.
I leave with pills and advice
to
    'Wee after sex and wipe front to back.'

Good Girls Swallow

I imagined
Dr Clinical wore paisley pyjamas.
They were 100% silk and he had eggs Benedict for breakfast.
Dr Clinical read the Daily Mail in the morning,
tugging at the threads of his Freudian couch,
yawning.

That morning,
I
roll out of bed,
          crawling
          from my
               room

                    to
                    the tap.
                    I drown in cold water.
I down litres
and clench my pelvic floor tight on the journey to see Dr Clinical,
who's early,
inspecting my notes from his jury.

I sit in the waiting room, burying my envy into the thigh gap of
    the girl next to me.
My fingers tiptoe across my winning collar bones before Brown
    Boots the counsellor
drops the scales at my toes.

I step on
and the numbers in the tiny window flicker
like a stripper teasing punters with a flash under knickers.
Brown Boots marks down the final figure.

In Dr Clinical's office, I sink into my school sweatshirt
as he peers over his glasses at the spreadsheet of my statistics.
Brown Boots is next to me, clutching her notes.

She clears her throat and says,
>'She just says *I don't know* to my questioning. She won't tell me anything.'

Dr Clinical sighs
as my digital polygraph validates that I've not been swallowing as much as I promised him
and, again, I am threatened with medical incarceration.
Well, it's that or I'll die if I carry on the way I'm going.

Back in the fishtanked institute of learning, I attempt to kill my mental hindrance with a biscuit.
Swallowing like a good girl, it's not long before I'm choking on remorse.
I hang my head over the toilet bowl near the dinner hall
and I resurrect my sins with force, pouring turning fingers down my throat.
Wearing splashback on my forehead,
I wipe my two fingers,
glazed and dripping in ginger nut gelatine.

I turn up late to IT.
The teacher takes his opportunity to take me out into the corridor.
Like a virus, he uses me to host his desires and 'accidentally glances'
down my shirt.
He tells me to button up to the top and that his class is
too hard to teach when he's distracted by me.
Swallowing.
I do as I'm told, like a good girl, and he whispers, 'You're special.'

i learnt to be small

in   those

              i learnt
              to be
              small

four   walls

Get the Junkie Look

I knew I was still fucked
when I looked at the junkie stumbling down Noel Street
and envied his skeletal legs and protruding ribs.

beds

the mad woman in the attic

she comes in the dead of the night
in the eye of a flame
and dull scents
of ancient wood-fired smoke
she lingers in the doorway

wires of black tendrils
obscure her face
as she crawls
in circles
in her red dress
fingernails long
she scrapes
shovels of skin and draws blood

in her sleep
her tongue clicks
before her release
deep rumbles
of escaped cackles
through stale breath
and into sore eyeballs

we waited on my bed

I picked at the green nail varnish that had hardened on the sheets
and her cheeks were lily white
and he was down the alley with blood in his eyes

time went slow on my bed
ears pricked at sirens
shadowed lenses lay cracked in the alley
and shackled rage bled in justice over his face

my veins were busy
under skin ridged in goosebumps
our feet were bare
and hung limp off the side of my bed
dripping heat onto the floor

we waited on my bed
after he got away
our bodies loaded in his camera
and I whispered to her
don't worry
dad will kill him

no tummy aches tonight, please

I spent my whole childhood with a tummy ache. A twisting pain born from anxiety that left me writhing most the time and I hid it. I was bold. People thought I was self-assured but, poor girl, I swallowed razor-edged butterflies every night. I would sink fingernails into my thighs and smiled when they fluttered. I was scared of the unknown. Like sleeping where the darkness looks different. The dark always looks different in someone else's room. Where dressing-gown ghosts are a different shade and disguise behind crooked hoods to sniff new prey. The nighttime spied, licked dry eyes, and my breath would spend the whole night hitting its head off my chest. My overnight bag would brim as full as my eye bags. Tiredness crooked from sleepless nights. The tea cooked by mums would sit funny in my tummy. The thought of chocolate made me sick, and the sweets I would eat to look normal clawed at me. I mimicked ghost stories, scouting screams through the bobble-ended blankets. I dampened the pleas to stop from the wuss girl in the corner by saying it's only a story. When they slept, I would hold the note from my sister that said she loved me, and no tummy aches tonight please.

Madonna

My sister hated the gap in her front teeth
and my mum said
she should love it
because Madonna had a gap in her teeth
and everyone loves Madonna.
We clapped
under the bramble bush on the landing.
Mum sat
in front of her pine dressing table
on the matching pine chair
wrapped with a green velvet back.
Her fringe was pulled away from her face
by the black and white foundation-stained hairband
and she smelt like Nivea face cream.
Routine
was where my mum sat comfortably,
nestled safely in familiarity.
Her hair drawer was jammed
full of rollers wrapped in runaway strands
and the air was stained with burnt hair
singed in the dryer's cracked diffuser.
I bit the nail varnish lid
that was glued
shut tight with spillage
and my teeth tingled,
jaw drilling
to ease the fixed sticking.
We painted our nails
gloopy pink
and raided Mum's jewellery box
that sat next to the toxic mousse
and tea stain drops.
We dripped in her chunky gold hoops and chains
and then balanced on our shoulders
on the bed
with our legs in the air.

We wrapped ourselves in Mum's underwired bras
and drowned in her silky slips,
lips
over-lined with her blunted rose liner.
I swear
we looked like Madonna.

dirty stop-out

girls are built by society
to
brush it off

ourselves
others
she was too drunk
she asked for it

it was only a squeeze
an unwanted touch
these things happen

we've seen girls
passed out

being fucked
too gone
to even put on her own knickers
it happened to her
it's been me
when I was sixteen

I woke up
after being violated
I went to school
unwashed
it was me
I forgot my book
and fell asleep
my teacher asked me
where I had been
I hadn't been home yet
she looked at me
like I was filth
dirty stop-out
she called me
out
they say our girls should be taught
boundaries

shame

                is weaved
     through our bodies
            how can we believe we are worthy
when the women who teach us
          see boys touch us
               but look
                 through it

    and tell us
that's just how it is
        boys have needs
            you better
          get used to it
   be careful
         or get used
     it's not their fault
it's up to you
to protect yourself

Sick Night

When did the sign of a good night become
a burning throat
and a cramping stomach?

Muscles squeezing
to force the vomit
of the familiar, bitter liquid
that fizzes, then settles
into the water at the bottom of the toilet?

At what point do we forget the nights we've spent
shutting our eyes
to still feel like we're lurching,
stunned in the blinking strobes with the stomping beat?

When will we stop having nights that end
with a cracked iPhone
and scuffed white trainers splattered in mud?

Our legs covered in unexplainable bruises,
mascara-stained cheeks,
and strip eyelashes discarded and curled on the floor?

In My Bed

I've got bed head at the moment.
My alarm clock goes off,
but
the truth takes refuge in my clean sheets
and makes them musty.

4am

i can feel the fat on my arms. fuck.
i can feel the fat on my arms. fuck.
i can feel the fat on my arms.
i can feel the fat on my arms.
i can feel the fat on my arms.
i can feel the fat.
i can feel the fat.
i can feel the fat.
i can feel the fat.
i feel fat.
i feel fat.
i feel fat.
i feel fat.
i feel fat.
i can feel.
i can feel.
i can feel.
i can feel.
i can feel.
i can feel.
i can feel.
i can feel.
i can feel.
i can feel.
i can feel.
i can feel.
and i don't want that.

heads

skin

itchy
mottled
clusters

white
j i t   e   r y threads
    t

peachy
cloud
lighter
burns

luminous
satin
saucers

crater
spattered
cheeks

p   p
r   a
e   r
c   a
i   l
s   l
e   e
l   l
y
s
l
i
t

zippy

I didn't shut up as a kid   I was told I was
too much
too loud
        that I needed to learn when to shut up
all the time
and I just couldn't stop talking
I couldn't think long enough before I spoke which was another
    thing I was always told think before you speak but it wasn't
    me and I felt like zippy from rainbow that I needed my mouth
    zipped by other people because I had no control over the
    flapping fabric jaw on my face and
I should be more like george the hippo
he was a nice little hippo
thing
and it was that bloody zippy that did everyone's head in and didn't
    know when to shut up I didn't know when to shut up and I
    didn't know when I should speak
and I started to hate the sound of my own voice
                                                    I was too much
people didn't want to hear me and were probably going to hate
    me if I spoke
too much
or said the wrong thing and if you have nothing nice to say you
    should say nothing and I didn't seem to know what was nice
    to say and what was not so maybe I should say nothing but I
    couldn't say nothing because it wasn't me so

        I'll just starve myself instead

Porridge, Cream & Syrup

The Lyle's golden syrup tin at my gran's stood on the kitchen table,
dressed in gilded pathways of mornings past.
The belly of the porridge bulged proudly in the middle of the bowl
and the cream settled as a cold white moat around the rim.
The sucrose adhesive on Lyle's lid meant my gran had to
prise it open.
   'You take the spoon,
    explore the tin of gold,
      and if it spills

         don't worry.
          There can
           never
            be too
             much.'

alcopops and corner shops

we lived in a branded land. an average town run by kids
sporting jd sports bags at school. we smoked richmond
superking on the hill by the pool. we shared nudges online.
one prod too many. spammed. had us whipping off our tops
on webcam. our bodies were shared on motorola razrs. we
smoked weed in sheds. in lessons we blasted smack that and
sat patiently whilst lads touched us up. we ground the fruities
in the chicken shops for the men behind the counters. we gave
blow jobs. in the park. and that was filmed too. in the dark.
we stayed alive by downing frosty jack's, aftershock. shoulder
marks lingered. fingernails dug in. faking orgasms we'd never
had. lying back, clawing backs, whilst they'd pound. arses
smacked. mimicked porn screams. reviving energy from cans.
dodging dodgy-looking vans. ignoring leers from a dodgy-
looking man. doing doggy where we can. we chased the
chaser. intoxicated, labelled wasters. socially safer. wearing
mckenzie under blazers.

getting fucked by a junkie

nothing seduces me like the
alluring taste of
exposed bones
a shrinking waist
and the temptation of shedding just one more stone
you charm your way back inside me
uninvited but not unwelcomed
blasted tip
forced before I'm ready
and time again you pop the cherry
you hit the spot like no other
the creeping touch of screaming hunger
launching me to heights of euphoric wonder
I suffer without you
in the gorging of thoughts
I feel too much
but you sort it
because there's nothing more seductive to me
than feeling
nothing

Forgive Me, Father, for I Have Synned

The Slimmers 5.15

People dressed in Sunday best, ready to watch the wetting of the
   baby's head
over conversations of skipping breakfast in bed.
That morning, they sing hymns and cite prayers promising to
   teach this baby right from wrong
in honour of Jesus Christ as the Son of God.
In ill-fitted attire, a slimmer parades proudly, claiming her
   waistband is loose
after weigh-in day in the local leisure centre's spare room.
The slimmers wade past pews and walk through to the connecting
   village hall,
ready to deny grains in front of other females who say,
   'Oh, not for me, thank you, I'm being good.'
They finger the linen tablecloth awkwardly, connecting uncertain
   glances through crevices,
then they walk away from it, faking effortless willpower, the
   slimmer's holy writ.
Led into temptation, a sinner watches the vultures savage a plate
of syns and says,
   'OK. I'll just have a small piece of cake, then…
   and one pork pie…
   oh dear, now I haven't been good.
   So, yes, I might as well have a glass of wine.
   I'll start again on Monday and I'll be better next time.'

I overdosed on pain relief

the pain relief packet
mass-produced packed poison
waits patiently
on the white table in front of me
I hang up the phone
and my heart aches at the fate determined by the voice from
the triple digits
of
one
one
one
my last coin is spent and my palms are outstretched
approved and assessed
hands now full of bleached white pills
the final binge to obscure all reality
three more digits are gambled
and shame is spoken to another stranger
I leave
empty-handed
penniless poor

uniformed compassion wires up a pager
a home invasion
and I'm taken to wait for a bed in the hospital
there are no beds
my sins stain the floor
left to crouch by a door
nameless faces glance over
and I'm instructed to pour
the thick, black liquid
down into my system
choking on
the charcoal reverse
from the overworked nurse
my mouth is stained black

a shamed joker smile across my cheeks
more wires
and needles
are attached
they tell me to
relax
but my veins are pulsing with pain that I can't explain
when it's time
to look into the eyes
of the woman
who gave me life

mentally disordered persons found in a public place

the cold breeze stirs in a home that's not my own. old carpet
scratching under my thighs
leaving blotches. ink spilt. water-coloured skies.
I trace the hollows of my body with my fingertips and I'm sniped
at by that rogue something who lives in there with me.
follow.
I crawl bleary-eyed down the safety plan steps. snap the elastic
band on my wrist. a healthy swap for skin slits.
twist
the bath taps. and sink sins in remedy oil. then shiver in a towel
on the floor by the toilet. I force morning bile up. part
compulsion. part routine. I
scrabble
for my notebook and pen to unburden fog into words. I don't
want to be here anymore. I watch my scrawls scramble into
instruction.
your end. go get it.
I fear faces. and relate to the faceless. find comfort in bright light
escorts. see only those who have passed on. in the decluttered
future my time here is finished. I was best before. time-tripped.
past my use-by date.
you hurt for happiness.
steps wink from graffiti scrawls. luring me to the end of the sky. the
truth stretched over tarmac miles.
I swallow   blasts   of   air   on the bridge.
I lean over the edge and
I don't flinch.

999
is called
without me knowing

and sirens blast down malbourne way.
I jitter. hopscotch
left   to   right
and back up onto railings.

down the bridge.

I see one. I run. my heels are clipped by cars cutting the streets. a near miss. there are cracks in the concrete. I can't turn. there's a copper behind the fence. grabbing at getaway ankles. and the uniformed border coaxes me.

I fight.

I beat their armour with my limbs.

their grasps tighten and grip my skin. hunted.

in between each breath of my mind's whirlwind. thrashing about like a newborn shooting palms for their first grasp.

I drop.

to the pavement for my escape. swing my bodyweight. ten officers. bind my wrists. they drag me to their van and lock the cell.

they arrest me.

they arrest me. when I'm already so trapped in my head. the cold tin shrinks around my brain. my screams hang like a lead-footed lump in my neck. I beat the pen with feathered fists. in the dark. I gain new bruises. from each bump in the road. hope has grown too heavy for my hands to hold. I let go.

and a hand reaches me in my cell.

Fulbourn

My mum told me about that place

    'It's haunted.' She paused.
    'Grandad hated it.'
And I'd seen him that morning, in the light of the sun,
floating like a stray star above the motorway.
He was just hanging around the door to my dizzy new home, or
    something close.
I was still screaming out the half-door of the cell
at the copper who told me they were taking me to Fulbourn.
    'She had electric shock treatment there,
    his mum,
    and he came home and broke down crying after seeing her.'
He said he'd let me up front
if I calmed the fuck down.
I held my breath in the back of the van,
wrists like paper, I twisted the cuffs to freedom but they just
    tightened.
The officers burnt a journey in gas and I sank like an echo in the
    back.
I wilted in the tree shadows at the temporary traffic lights outside
    the place.
    'They didn't treat them properly in them days.'
The gates loomed
and the van drove us in and all I could think about was that scene
    in *Shawshank* when they drop off fresh meat
and the path was long and winding.
I started to feel attached to the officers that had decided my fate
    was Fulbourn,
like every morning before school
when I would cling to my mum and scream,
unsure of the unknown.
The two workers stood outside the high caged courtyard and knew
    my name.
They reminded me of a ghostly butler and maid
working all hours,
dead and haunting.

I thought about running
but remembered the cuffs around my wrists and was coerced in
when they spoke my name in kind tones
and plastered smiles between their cheeks.
My hands dried into fists.
Nails sinking into my palms as footsteps chattered holes in the
floor.
From outside in
they showed me around.
Soft walls.
Half doors.
Padded plastic furniture. They offered me the bed,
to which I said
no.

    'Other people had her clothes.
    He went in there one day to see her and someone else had
    her slippers on.'

The pale ghosts locked themselves in another room with glass
    away from me.
They tapped on laptops.
And the female coppers tapped on laptops.
And I pulled my legs up on the plastic sofa and froze.
The haunted house scratched at me.
I was left with only crumbs of my dark thoughts and their
    constant tapping.
Tap.
Tap.
I asked where the toilet was.
Tap.
The old blonde officer said she'd have to come in with me
    in case I tried anything
silly.
Tap.
Tap.
On the toilet my head screamed at the half door and left
    chattered teeth in the padded block.
The doctors journeyed to assess and the coppers left.
Don't go, I thought.
Hours fell around the noisy caged walls.

Professionals took shifts.
And the psychologists appeared, clutching the end of the
    motorway in their notes.
They sat far away from me.
Like I had sharp teeth, or something close.
I stayed curled on the plastic furniture,
my skin dirty, torn numb.
Shredded from attempted escape from those damn cuffs.
There were three of them, dressed in suits,
asking me questions,
but the only one that mattered was
do you still want to die?
    'She never came out of there,
    his mum.'
No,
I answered,
and they sent me home in a taxi that I wanted to jump out of.

bunnies

I sat in the field
where the myxomatosis bunnies once froze
and didn't cry
you came across with despair in your eyes
and the cliff crumbled like biscuits
under your feet
I couldn't lock the window
and you couldn't scratch time

the mad woman in my room

they said I was / only safe if nothing was mine / not space / not sleep / not time / they tried / to take everything from me / that could hurt me / but left my shoelaces / and I used them to tie my hair up / that first night / I was woken hourly / by the heavy door / opening / and two people / staring / backlit by the corridor light / my heart ran / every hour / they could easily / have me in this bed / with my name above it / and no one would know / I went stiff / like a child / confined / my skin / stuck to the / blue and plastic mattress / with the undersheet crumpled / from my wriggling / and turning / I woke up after their / last checks / to the breakfast alarm / and wailing outside my window / old mascara clung to my eyelashes / and my eyes stung / I sneaked a look / through the tinted window in my room / to see her / the woman wailing / she was the maddest of us all / kissed the hardest by disorder / or was it because / she was older / and had her lips planted on / the most / she chuntered / and blasted screams / bare feet / on concrete / bra-free / checked nightie / and navy cardie / I was wearing the / pyjamas in the same NHS check / and I ripped them off / I'm not as mad / as that / but I wasn't allowed out / before eight for a fag / and I was checked on / just as much / I got a bag of stuff dropped off / and they took it / I had to ask permission / for my foundation / for my lighter / to use my charger / I didn't eat the toast / at breakfast / pre-heated cardboard / and butter sat on it / like a boat on the still sea / I gave all my meals / to the mad woman / she would just eat / and eat / processed meat / the next night / I lent her a lighter / and she said thanks / then screamed at me an hour later / for nicking her lighter / the blokes moaned / each day / that the mad woman / had been going into their rooms / in the day / and whilst they slept at night / the third night / a girl came out the doctor's office / doped up to the eyeballs / eyes hazed / I asked them / to give some to me / but they gave me / promethazine / to make me sleep / after I took a plastic knife / from the kitchen / I had got used to the night checks now / and slept through the strangers / staring at me dream / they left my door open / after two o'clock checks / the promethazine night

52

/ and the mad woman came in / she swished / in her nightie /
and stood right over me / I heard her moans / and I watched her
sway / in my sedated state / the mad woman was in my room /
I walked her to the door / shut it / her meds started to work the
next morning / and she got her hair / french plaited / by one of
the nurses / and she put on a long red dress / and we told her
/ she looked nice / she didn't smile / but she was calmer / and
I saw her / as just a woman / for the first time / and I realised /
that we are mad / really / it's just what we choose to hide / and
what people see

I Am the Cat

My dawn was wrapped in Vacutainer needles
and piles of consent forms.
In specimen bags and gauzes,
antiseptic applauses from the doctor's pity pauses.
Carrying my life like a prescription penned script,
abbreviated for cordial consumption,
I'm caged in my sterile retreat.
I undress myself slowly from my baggy jumper and jeans,
unlace my Docs
and stand barefoot, like a corpse.
A daddy long legs,
an angel in the night,
I walk naked over to the hospital pyjamas.
The trousers bandage my slashed stomach
and I button the top over my bare breasts, the same,
grimacing as the fabric notices them.
My dawn is interrupted by strange men and women
flinging the locked door open to check I'm still living.
It was veiled in the early morning wake-up calls
of Alice's rage-fuelled howls
and it was shrouded
when the crumpled butterfly stuck on my window sighed.
It was cradled by overstretched systems
and facilitated by underpaid wages;
my existence lay futile
in front of the panel, a statistic.
I wait in line for my diagnosis and med prescription.
Handed it in a paper cup,
a solution for their omission,
I'm required to trade in my own submission.
I first felt my dawn break
when broken people nurtured hope through strings.
Souls wide open to songs of mended wings,
birds that sing,
moonbeams
and rainbow dreams.

Harmonious in harmony and spellbound in humanity,
smiles were formed through cracks shaped tirelessly
and wistful tears were shed heartily.
Damaged memories, muted black and white surrendered,
lay dormant
past tides pressed tender, and collective sunrises rose together.
My dawn was tomorrow's world,
it was fires for the cold
and, that day,
I left the stray cats
and copycats,
wild cats
and fat cats
howling in the dark shadows.
Inhaling smoke into my own carved dawn,
I am the cat that walks alone.

Acknowledgements

Eternal gratitude to Karen for being the first person to hear me. For teaching me insight and worth. For modestly showing me kindness, patience and support like no other. For being the stability for me to carry on. This book is for you.

My thanks to Metal Culture for the continual guidance, opportunity and funding for this book to exist. In particular to Sarah, Ruth and Jack for your truly valued support. Also to Charley, Keely and Sandy for your assistance, time and incredible insight.

To everyone at Burning Eye Books, in particular Bridget for your hard work and invaluable advice in guiding this process.

To my parents for giving me freedom, trust and independence. My mum for giving me your heart and head that doesn't stop whirring. My dad for your enlightenment and your unwavering curiosity and my sister, Amy, for being the only other person to see through my eyes. For your strength, acceptance and understanding. To my Gran for providing the security of love and warmth to us all and to my grandad for his imagination and everlasting impact. To Hannah and Chloe for being my constant. Thank you for your loyalty, love and lighthearted relief in life.

With love and gratitude to my selfless, gentle and carefree Tom for providing me with unconditional strength. You are my safe place. To our joyful, bright, inquisitive wildflower, Daisy. Let your light continue to shine brightly. You will always be heard